S. Twdgill

Brian Patten was born in Liverpool in 1946,
was educated at a local secondary modern school
and for the last six or seven years has earned a
living through his writing.
A main contributor to the revival of oral
poetry in England, he left Liverpool some years
ago and has since moved from place to place. His
poems have been widely published in newspapers
and magazines as well as in *Penguin Modern
Poets*. He has also read many of his poems on
television and radio.
In 1967 his first collection, *Little Johnny's
Confession,* was published by Allen & Unwin
and *Notes to the Hurrying Man* followed in 1969.
An L.P., *Brian Patten Reading His Poetry,* was
recently issued by Caedmon and *The Elephant And
the Flower,* his first book of children's stories,
was published by Allen & Unwin in 1970.

D1585964

NOTES TO THE HURRYING MAN

by Brian Patten
LITTLE JOHNNY'S CONFESSION
THE ELEPHANT AND THE FLOWER
THE IRRELEVANT SONG

NOTES TO THE HURRYING MAN

POEMS, WINTER '66 – SUMMER '68

by Brian Patten

London. George Allen and Unwin Ltd

First published in 1969
Second impression 1969
Third impression 1969
Fourth impression 1969
Fifth impression 1970
Sixth impression 1971

This book is copyright under the Berne Convention.
All rights reserved. Apart from any fair dealing for the purpose
of private study, research, criticism or review, as permitted
under the Copyright Act, 1956, no part of this publication may
be reproduced, stored in a retrieval system, or transmitted, in
any form or by any means, electronic, electrical, chemical,
mechanical, optical, photocopying, recording or otherwise,
without the prior permission of the copyright owner. Enquiries
should be addressed to the Publishers.

© Brian Patten, 1969

ISBN 0 04 808005 5 cloth
ISBN 0 04 808007 1 paper

Printed in Great Britain
in Univers type
by Compton Printing Ltd, London and Aylesbury

ACKNOWLEDGEMENTS

Some of these poems have previously appeared
in a number of underground magazines and broad-
sheets and in *The Scotsman, The Sunday Times,
London Magazine, The Quarterly Review of
Literature* and *Transatlantic Review.* 'Into My Mirror
Has Walked' first appeared in *Love, Love, Love*
(Corgi Books) and 'Sad Adam' was first published
in a limited edition by Turret Books. 'A Small Dragon'
and 'The Rockinghorse' were commissioned by
the Barrow Poets. Other poems have been
broadcast by the B.B.C. and some taped for
the Harvard University poetry library.
To all who took an interest in them, my thanks.

CONTENTS

INTO MY MIRROR HAS WALKED

Into my mirror has walked
A woman who will not talk
Of love or of its subsidiaries,
But who stands there,
Pleased by her own silence.
The weather has worn into her
All seasons known to me,
In one breast she holds
Evidence of forests,
In the other, of seas.

I will ask her nothing yet
Would ask so much
If she gave a sign—

Her shape is common enough,
Enough shape to love.
But what keeps me here
Is what glows beyond her.

I think at times
A boy's body
Would be as easy
To read light into,
I think sometimes
My own might do.

NOW WE WILL EITHER SLEEP, LIE STILL, OR DRESS AGAIN

Evening and the sun warming the bird
in her cupped hands.
Over the room's silence other voices and sounds.
My love, the world is a distant planet

... and bending here you are naked,
wind from the half open skylight hardens breasts,
your blonde hair falling is spread across me.
The bird in your cupped hands rising.

Let our touchings be open;
We do not belong to a race of pale children
whose bodies are hardly born
nor among the virgins hung still inside their sadness,
but waking in strange beds we are screwed and perfect.

Littered about the room still
are the clothes we wore while meeting.
Evening and the sun has moved across the room.
Now we will either sleep, lie still, or dress again.

THE TELEPHONISTS
The Engineer's Dream

He dreams
Of the secret ways they would lay him,
Of the worried gardens, the old ruins where they would take him
The pale girls
who never blush at the jokes he tells them
He dreams
For how can he imagine them anything other than beautiful
The young telephonists
Tuned into cities
Whose bodies receive and send out messages
Who travel down the warm long wires
To where something tender is being said

How difficult not to answer
The whispering voices
The hurried confessions
The first sentence broke at its centre
The last question left unanswered
How difficult to imagine
The girl three months pregnant
Who stumbling out her coded message
Breaks down, asks
Can you exterminate a generation?
And how with one quick call
Dreams can be aborted
And birds dozing on the wires tainted—
Through silence only the good messages go unheard
Stopping though the wires continue—

How can he imagine them
Anything other than beautiful
Those girls

Whose heads are jammed with the city's secrets
And yet how can he imagine
Their own bodies' failure
Or how easily they are lost and
The long wires sing
Of their own situations.

THE PROJECTIONIST'S NIGHTMARE

This is the projectionist's nightmare :
A bird finds its way into the cinema,
finds the beam, flies down it,
smashes into a screen depicting a garden,
a sunset and two people being nice to each other.
Real blood, real intestines, slither down
the likeness of a tree.
'This is no good,' screams the audience,
'This is not what we came to see.'

OLD CROCK

I am the very last astronaut, listen:
I send back messages from obscure planets;
smoke rises from the burning leaves,
something goes liquid beyond my reach.

I am the very last astronaut, listen:
I came here, surfacing like a whale
through oceans alchemists made real.

Listen: space-bugs scrape around the cockpit,
terror leaks in, spilling about the controls;
lice block the air tubes, eat into my brain.

I have forgotten my space pills, I
might explode.

About the brain: most is machinery anyway.
No worry there; only the memory now
feels soft and edible.

My only fear: that the lice might nest there,
eat out the shapes I've carried with me.
Still now I sense my loneliness breaking.

Now someone else has arrived here,
space-jaunted naked, sits invisible here.
I'm obsolete, he tells me, holds up a mirror.

I am the very last astronaut, listen:
skull-white I grin,
skull-white and obviously mad.

Outside there are children playing
like this blackness were a park,
dancing, their songs numerical—

I am too many centuries old.

In the brain-pan bits of machinery float,
still active, trying to get out the holes
where my eyes have been.

IT IS ALWAYS THE SAME IMAGE

It is always the same image;
of you wandering naked out from autumn rivers,
your body steaming, covered with rain,
blue and grey drops fall from you,
when you speak
leaves fall and disintegrate.

It is always the image of your breasts,
full of the violence of seaplants
that quiver when touched; fish
mate beneath you; your body blue, your
shadow following,
both seen like ghosts from distant promenades
by a fearful audience.

The same image
but now a lake surrounded by ferns,
and just visible through the mist
a thousand lovers following you naked
leaving no traces in the corners of dawn.

AND PERHAPS WHERE HE IS

And perhaps on another planet, on one
not quite as near as ours to the sun,
there is a man with an overcoat up tight
around his face, happy listening
as his breath turns to ice and fills
the ground with tiny stars.

And perhaps he is further from our version of tenderness,
is one who likens himself to a world
floating further from the sun
and where because of this all creatures sense
how cold it's grown and what that coldness has done.

Above where he is
men in their silver coffins spin
some tender and some untender myth.

Perhaps where he is
further from a public world than us
he has learnt to make all worlds his own,
his tenderness too huge for one.

And perhaps where he is
only loving rockets can land and only good men
get out and shake his hands.

DIARY POEM

We sit here, twenty ; drunk. Wind and stars
gush in through the skylight. We sense
in the air how winter's coming
and how our lives and those that surround them
have frozen. We sit, neither sane nor mad,
outside in a room we'll never enter
our first crime, a child, bawls out,
shakes a fist in anger. Inside us
sad and lonely creatures wander,
looking for an exit from themselves. They
are more important now than the shapes we wear.
Those shapes are not unique.

We have sent out frantic messages, covering
the city, all its men, its women.
Yet those few who came forward did not move us.
Confined by faith to a flower that's perishing
we move, frozen not by these seasons
but by our own weather. It's inside us
that the years pour.

Then perhaps it is best that we wake expecting little,
feel no more need to exaggerate ourselves
nor perform those rituals that have ceased to amaze us,
but washed by the morning's first light
to drift out into the city, one thought
in its still sleeping brain. . . . And yet
on waking we find
that longing for something other than our own shapes
grows continually, eats away at all other things till
one seemingly unperishable thing is left—
it is the need of each other, is love
the bruised shape we pick
from now freezing orchards.

Winter 1966

18

YOU COME TO ME QUIET AS RAIN
NOT YET FALLEN

You come to me quiet as rain not yet fallen
afraid of how you might fail yourself your
dress seven summers old is kept open
in memory of sex, smells warm, of boys,
and of the once long grass.
But we are colder now; we have not
love's first magic here. You come to me
quiet as bulbs not yet broken
out into sunlight.

The fear I see in your now lining face
changes to puzzlement when my hands reach
for you as branches reach. Your dress
does not fall easily, nor does your body
sing of its own accord. What love added to
a common shape no longer seems a miracle.
You come to me with your age wrapped in excuses
and afraid of its silence.

Into the paradise our younger lives made
of this bed and room
has leaked the world and all its questioning
and now those shapes terrify most
that remind us of our own. Harder now
to check longings or sentiment, to care overmuch,
you look out across years, come to me
quiet as the last of our senses closing.

THE TRANSLATION
A Song

Lady it is evident by the rain gathering in your eyes
how easily our loving
has translated into pain
and from its nest among moments
a slow, sad bird has flown,
it perches on my words
and sings this refrain:

'From my nest among moments
Where I keep a spinning world
I stole one crumb of joy
But lost it coming here.'

Lady it is evident by the rain gathered in your eyes
how puzzled by a sudden loss
the world disintegrates,
and when it's done with loving
the heart breaks into squares,
it floats behind your eyes
and it gibbers everywhere:

'From my nest among moments
Where I keep a spinning world,
I stole one crumb of joy
But lost it coming here.'

THE PROPHET'S GOOD IDEA

A new prophet appeared recently; was first seen
walking out an ocean. Which? We've forgotten.

            He said
to the hushed crowds that had gathered, to
the journalists, the radio and television newscasters,
the Look at Life team and the politicians:
        'Stay in Bed.'
That was his message. 'Bring each other
cups of coffee;
lie naked as near as possible without touching,
think of governments, chewing-gum, wars,
Queen Elizabeth coronation cups, anything—
you're bound finally to burst out laughing.
Draw peace maps across each others bodies.
Climb into bed. Imagine if everyone did.
Returning astronauts would hear
only the sound of dreaming.'

  Well the hushed crowds, the journalists, the
radio and television newscasters,
the Look at Life team and the politicians
thought it sounded a good message; a clear message,
the kind they could pass on
quite harmlessly to children.
Bed manufacturers were informed.
They loved the idea, loved it. Made beds big enough
to hold several hundred people
thinking of chewing-gum, Queen Elizabeth coronation cups,
                                  anything—
  'It sounds so good a message,' said the people,
'that something's bound to be wrong. . . .'
          So philosophers, house-hold names and a
                    TV personality

gathered to discuss the message. There were
a few flaws to be ironed out—
Robots were to be invented for the menial task
of running the planet—otherwise, a fine message.

And so now the whole planet's sleeping;
East and West snores, Hansel and Gretel personified.
Moss and moonwort burst out from bank-vaults;
all manner of creatures make themselves at home in houses;
from bed to bed spiders spin their webs, dream-catchers.
And there are sleep-walkers and sleep-lovers
in nightgowns or pyjamas, in underwear or nothing,
wandering through fields or suburbs, all so quietly.
And some woken from nightmares sit and comfort one another
whispering, *and o it's all madness* !

        And occasionally
the prophet rising from his ocean
drifts down the inland currents, watches whatever moves.
Occasionally drags himself up into radio-ships
where earphones to his brain he listens,
makes sure it is all still silent.
And o it's all madness and he has little else to do
him suffering from insomnia,
adrift in his faery-tale silence.

HAVING TAKEN THE NECESSARY PRECAUTIONS

Having taken the necessary precautions against
dream-birth we were allowed to lie together,
messing up each others lives till mixing
the mess became intolerable. And then my loves (if
I humorously might call you that) it was
the finger in the mouth or the stomach pump. Being
too polite to jump from buildings, fearing
the caretaker's wrath would reach heaven
and bug you still further, pills sufficed.

We never quite managed to kill each other though
some strange attempts were made;
even the most tender ones, their tonques red
lizards on spines, while together were suffocating
one less visible than themselves. Even those who
made gentleness a profession or art had something
about them that cancelled beauty. Anonymously we
sent warnings to ourselves, anonymously
we rejected each of them.

Flowers won't cover the hurts, the half-inch deaths
we pile up; a rose the size of two fists
won't cover a pinprick of hating. Dreams larger
than ourselves we killed, not wanting
our smallness measured against them. And like greenfly
between the half-folded petals of a world, we
sleeping near its centre, blind to its colours,
nibble the heart out of it, till bloated
we lie dreamless, mind-blown in its ruins.

MR JONES TAKES OVER

Look, the Jones have moved into Paradise!
They've built a house there,
laid down a road or two,
built several yachts for the garden,
two garages, one church with its plastic vicar.

I asked hopefully when the lease would expire.
'We paid in cash,' they smiled.

NOR THE SUN ITS SELLING POWER

They said her words were like balloons
with strings I could not hold,
that her love was something in a shop
cheap and far too quickly sold;

but the tree does not price its apples
nor the sun its selling power,
the rain does not gossip
or speak of where it goes.

24

PORTRAIT OF A YOUNG GIRL RAPED AT A SUBURBAN PARTY

And after this quick bash in the dark
You will rise and go
Thinking of how empty you have grown
And of whether all the evening's care in front of mirrors
And the younger boys disowned
Led simply to this.

Confined to what you are expected to be
By what you are
Out in this frozen garden
You shiver and vomit—
Frightened, drunk among trees,
You wonder at how those acts that called for tenderness
Were far from tender.

Now you have left your titterings about love
And your childishness behind you
Yet still far from being old
You spew up among flowers
And in the warm stale rooms
The party continues.

It seems you saw some use in moving away
from that group of drunken lives
Yet already ten minutes pregnant
In twenty thousand you might remember
This party
This dull Saturday evening
When planets rolled out of your eyes
And splashed down in suburban grasses.

PARK POEM

See how the lake, less active now, is silent;
sea creatures seen through a shoal of leaves
are swans still sleeping,
nesting where the leaves have frozen
and the soil is crusted over
with rain and with the memory of dawn.

And new minds that have cleared themselves of dreaming
see how in all weather
things are frozen to themselves,
and how in the spaces between each leaf
the swan's breath is moving
and its heart is beating against the clouds.

Grass, wind, earth, insects and senses agree
one wanderer lost deep inside his park
is free from names and personalities
among the frozen citizens of dawn.

GIRL IN A BLUE CARDIGAN

Watching you in city squares,
young, not noticeably pretty, blue cardigan
covering average breasts, hipster denim skirt
covering average hips; seventeen, known
as an average lay. Perhaps tomorrow
I might find myself becoming averagely involved.
A blue cardigan, one button undone, soon
all might burst open. Clerks
turn to face you when you move from benches; slow girl
stretching across lawns; walking, hands on imaginary balls,
the lunchtime ambition of a thousand commuters.
School finished with you wander about cafés
where the young blond musicians sit whispering
Blow-job blow-job, she's blow-job
Guitarist from Mike's group
taught her how to plate correctly.
Known to each of them
On such afternoons invitations, rooms
have but one identity,
and this afternoon you wander freely.
They have been with you who is
anyone disguised as one,
come too quickly beneath railway bridges disappointing you,
slowly in the Sunday parks, the happier shiverings of those
who are anyone disguised as one.
And I have wandered likewise
a bedroom-headed boy bored by polite touchings,
have made you manfood—
who one spring ago was terrified to be touched
now does the touching.

In afternoon squares
blue cardigans blooming, buttons
glittering in the sunlight.

A RAFT OF APPLES

Born into rivers of light rain; were
we on a raft of apples first
or perhaps at the edge of a clearing
where through mist we saw
small creatures eat their ways into dawn?

From separate sleeps into one waking
how red a raft of apples floating.
With ropes of wind we will harness dawningales
to pull us across a country of love;
when flowers are hungry we will give them each
a cloud or two. Laughing like idiots
we turn logic into rain,
that this is an ordinary world
forever amazes us. Laughing,

we spin wide awake into ourselves,
stretch our hands deep into a world
not to catch or bring back anything,
but simply to feel how it moves
and how on our skin
the wind's life is planted.

NOTE TO THE HURRYING MAN

All day I sit here doing nothing but
watching how at daybreak
birds fly out and return no fatter
when it's over. Yet hurrying about this room
you would have me do something similar;
would have me make myself a place
in that sad traffic you call a world.
Don't hurry me into it; offer
no excuses, no apologies.
Until their brains snap open
I have no love for those who rush
about its mad business;
put their children on a starting line and push
into Christ knows what madness.

You will not listen.
'Work at life!' you scream,
and working I see you rushing everywhere,
so fast most times you ignore
two quarters of your half a world.
If all slow things are useless
and take no active part in nor justify your ignorance
that's fine; but why bother screaming after me?
Afraid perhaps to come to where I've stopped
in case you find
into some slow and glowing countryside
        yourself escaping.
Screams measure and keep up the distance between us:
        Be quieter—
I really do need to escape;
take the route you might take
if ever this hurrying is over.

29

NOTE WHILE WALKING HOME

Walking home late, watched by all manner of things but
by nothing human; tree bark's glowing,
almost rain falling. My friends all in cities,
in Liverpool, in London, phoning
maybe loving, perhaps
wondering what to do this evening.
Rain that's not reached me yet
might fall on their roofs now,
mist up the bus windows behind which they are dreaming.
Here I wonder at how lives so invisible link,
touched by a common weather,
at how in the gap time makes between
hello and loneliness
memory teems; drenches.
Wandering home late
what I know of each separate person melts,
forms such feelings I can express no better than
the wind that moves across me will.

PARTY NOTES

The young pop-singers, newly mystical,
stand round smoking pot,
an ugly girl tinkles her bells wondering
about all that's not happened to her;
the poets, too tired for erections,
for flowers; the servants, lonely steppenwolves
moon reflecting in their silver trays;
the clowns, the acrobats,
the dead planet found in the fountain.
The host is already asleep. His children
dream dreams they have wished on themselves.
And the wife screwed in the basement
and the daughter in the attic
brown legs spread open and raised
waits fearfully for Sunday's obscene reporters
to come and throw slime over the occasion.

NOTES ON MY FRIENDS

Stunted trees in my friends back-gardens; their children
bawling in attics, in wooden crates
the never used belongings; bags stuffed
with letters and books, with notes informing of
various arrivals. Mattresses sprawled across floors—
sleeping near the ground still my friends
work hard at being human. Boy friends,
their faces pale, high cheek-bones that speak of beauty,
long fingers touching all that is real.
And lovers half-naked in kitchens,
white and brown bodies singing at breakfast,
dress each other in gentleness, act out their dreams as only
woken dreamers may. Hecketty, breasts pressed against
windows, lets dawn wash her; always surprised
at bird-song her brother turns on the recorder.
Mary, for all her lovers, lets the phone ring forever.
Some happy in dance halls, other in forests,
some in centrally-heated rooms, others in attics—
I smell them risen from all manner of sleeping;
tins of beans or continual restaurants,
concerned or not concerned with what's happening,
wandering through towns or cities and always time following,
each witness to the other's living, to their numerous dyings—
They seem more real now, grown more human,
deep into whatever ritual is left them.

MAROONED WHALES *

Now happier, we throw away the heavy words
 . . . like so many marooned whales
in sunlight their gloominess is absurd.
   What possible use?
      Imagine coming out your house
         and rushing into a favourite garden find
every leaf and colour crushed; find
         this stupid black whale wriggling about.

      You would need friends then
         to dig a hole deep enough to bury it
or love at least to obliterate it.

 . . . blow them away like they were dandelion seeds.
         We are light; our bodies
reflecting landscapes, our bodies mixed with rain,
   are light—why load them down?
      why make them clumsy, awkward?
There'll be enough time later;
         maybe later
everything will become a marooned whale! Maybe
birds will grow so fat you won't know the difference.
Imagine a sky full of marooned whales all singing
                     preposterous songs!

      Maybe our families even. . . .
   Huge whales in the living room
      knitting and watching television!

      When we eat an apple there in our hand
   will be this mad red whale. All the time, heavy like that,
                  we'd go crazy!

* This is a transcript of a poem improvised at a reading.

Be light awhile;
this skin is gentle, can laugh.
It's not always ridiculous.

　　　Maybe we have made too much of them
who found them very often
　　　　blocking our ways. Even
miles from oceans when we are miserable with each other
　　　'Hello' say the marooned whales.
　　　　　　And we find them
in other places than gardens;
in our beds when we are angry; find them in nightmares,
in car parks and cinemas;
in the public bar of the Crown and Anchor—
　　　　　　　　Anywhere.

Whales dressed in suits or beachwear, in overcoats or
pyjamas. Whales with umbrellas and whales with lunchboxes—
　　　Angry whale hitch-hikers
　　　　Whale politicians and whale poets
　　　　　　gloom gloom whales and mad whales

—belonging in oceans,
　　　light in oceans, happy even in oceans—
　　　　Misery is whale-meat.
　　　　I don't want to eat whale-meat.
I'm happy being a human picnic.
　　Whoever heard of a whale on a picnic?
I'll go mad thinking about marooned whales. . . .

SEEN THROUGH THE TREES BEHIND WHICH
YOU'RE WALKING

Seen through the trees behind which you're walking
that girl, soaking and pale,
and the boy running her to shelter
near where the suburbs fade.

Let them find there a makeshift bed
where they can lie and listen
to the thin rain teeming and city droning
near to where they've hidden.

She'll be young and he not much older,
their bodies come alive,
their time there will stand against
the closing down of dreams.

And both lying, drenched, dishevelled
in a time when their world's shrunk, gone stale,
they'll sense their loving on such days
open it a while.

For in some obscene future moment
something in them will have shrivelled
choked by the ignorant mind
that gives love a local duty.

Let them lie down together
and not with another's guilt,
let them touch as the rain touches
the world and all its shapes.

For as his hands rest now wet against her
so they'll rest in time
against the memory of a shelter
where they stopped once in the rain.

THE DREAM EXCHANGE

Financially unsuccessful as he was he liked running the place.
Crowds gathered to do business,
they'd push up against his counter each with a separate dream
and offering it they'd shout its value screaming
that the others were unreal.

There were dreams shaped like forests, a few
bright flowers, a few dull ones glowing;
there were some dreams pornographic, some
the density of oceans.
Some drifted, others needed parachutes.

One was shaped like a woman, tall and blonde and
damaged by boredom, she stood at the counter
dreamt up by a retired schoolmaster.
Someone else had dreamt a whale but couldn't
quite manage an ocean; another less ambitious
dreamt simply of grass. Queens came up offering
crowns studded with boys,
whores dreamt themselves innocent;
a priest wanted to exchange his question-marks.

He liked running the place;
cardboard boxes full of rainbows, marked 'perishable',
in the back room alchemists arranged their goods in lucky-bags.
He liked running the place; but the way
each shouted the other's dream down! the noise grew,
grew cracking his windows, the way they shouted,
screaming only of their own dream's value:
The shelves rotted when he touched them.
A bird made out of soil dipped its brain into a cloud.
The queen's dream undressed with the schoolmasters,
the only ones that made it they vanished laughing.

And now at the dream-exchange—
the price and value of each dream flickers through the tape
machines,
its worth diminishing as the crowd panics and panicking crushes
together.
In the back room, the alchemists, knowing the impossibility
of dreams mixing without peace, give up.
And the one who ran the place, pulling the shutters down
steps out over the remains of car crashes, over
fallen governments and half-submerged continents,
kicks a few stars out the way and decides
maybe to open up elsewhere or maybe not at all.

THE SONG

Bird song travels through gardens and reaches me.
For no particular reason I scoop up the song.
Once I would have sent it you
buried somewhere in cities
where fame and obscurities matter,
where dreams are eaten with breakfast.

But knowing I can do nothing but repeat in human terms
those truths we ourselves have made unworkable
I open my hands,
let the song free again.
Your ears might find it. Your eyes trap its source
between garden and walls.

Now I am lunatic enough to believe
elsewhere the song continues,
affects lives as equally as mine.
Presumptuous to offer as unique those things
we own in common; yet how common the heart
that without touching or wishing to own it,
lets the song nest there.

THROUGH THE TALL GRASS IN YOUR HEAD

Through the tall grass in your head
a grasshopper made out of stars is leaping;
It moves through those planets of information
Then leaves them behind it.
They'll soon explode.

You no longer bother watching how
Time and age leak down your mirror disfiguring it
Nor how that animal the centuries have tamed
Roams less restless now inside you.

You have reached that state
Where so much has ceased to matter
And outside your window you see that the garden too
Has grown weary of sunlight
And time has whittled down the cabbage leaves to thin white
                                                          wings.
All you did finally was to ask whether it was good.

THE MAGICIAN

Someone came into the room, told us
of a planet he had visited, a place
where dragons, elves, star-birds and angels
wandered, not always lovingly he said,
for even magic knew of panic,
but still they lived, they wandered;
and perhaps that planet's an inch from ours,
perhaps that's all it is but we
gossip of myth and hurry on.

Someone came into the room. In cupped hands
carrying what you thought was nothing, yet
in all the space between those palms
grew forests; all memory of nostalgia,
of hurt lip leaf touch and love was there
screwed in that cup of space between his fingers;
and though it was tight it
was loose and warm and wandered.

He was afraid and frightened by the mind
that discounting magic, had like a slug
lodged itself in some dull hole. And when you
went up to him and asked to be convinced
through the few sleeping senses you possessed
he simply asked through which of them you loved
and laughed, why split yourself into pieces,
you're small enough.

And in that room were some who knew his madness
larger than their sanity, who held
blurred memory of equal wonder.
Locked in their heads spun a similar planet,
but the air in which it spun was congested—

and you, whose knowledge is his presence
became arrogance, and who in place of wisdom
carried a dwarf, sat puzzled;
mind eye touch and smell
pressed against walls. Is imagination so dead you
can grow no larger?

RAUIN

A creature you will not bother to name
but that can name itself in anything
I push up through the stems of flowers
and step out on to lawns.
I am a star-swan, am newly-frozen rain
cracking under paws.
I am imagination; brushing against railings
they glow I leave
light in trees, know not whether
it is a lawn or universe I am crossing.
So be quieter my friends, do not
talk too much of me;
some vision of this planet might come and go
while you put into words my wonder.
I am whatever wakes you from comfortable beds
to come shivering
nightgowns around you
to press faces against freezing cloud.
And I am what you step towards in wonder,
the rainbow found breathing in bushes,
the first creature seeing through mists
new planets floating.
I follow the ant in its tree-trunk world.
I am imagination,
when I enter your women they glow;
you would pull curtains back on them that heaven
might see its only rival.
Are you watching me, here
with the lawns in your noses?
Whatever shape I take I will not
call you; I am silence,
in my immensity wander all your senses;
I am the paradise never lost only
you must evaporate before reaching me.

41

MAKING A CALL

Alone in a red phone booth escaping down the wires from myself
but never quite reappearing at the other end
where the warm fires and company of women tease loneliness,
add new dimensions, marshlands, to sadness.
An address book containing
its various memories of nakedness
fills out dullness, gives some hope but click!
down goes another phone.
Someone's just going out to dinner,
someone's too busy making money,
someone's just about to shoot himself!
All over cities people standing alone in red phone booths,
making frantic connections—
experts in communication
relating back to their own reflections in misted-up windows.
Why not just wait outside?
Ask the first to leave, Did you make a connection? No?
Then let's open lines to ourselves—
we want direct lines without mouthpieces,
want to work out new systems,
safeguards against our isolated wanderings.
Morning—telephone number sleeps with telephone number—
the rest recently woken from party floors, benches, bed-sitters,
shiver in the corners of tubes, buses,
wander down the paths of gatecrashed houses
—so tender to each other we stink!—
I dreamt one night the whole world slept together
                        in a red phone booth,
woke alone there. Laughed at my ridiculous situation.

THE LYRIC BIRD

And the lyric bird vomiting into blue air
falls back, its body shivering, wings broken.
Soon the sun will dry it out, insects gather.

Where did I first meet the lyric bird?
I met it at a skylight window or
in a garden among rusting pram wheels,
I met it soft beneath your dress.
Taking its shape from the earth's scents
I met the lyric bird in my head.

I sang with it for some time
and the lives around me
the sad lives
the brilliant lives
I ignored them.
I sang with the lyric bird.
It did not occur to me such birds can be amusing—
I was so glum!
It did not occur to me
its song might be
an echo of my own.

So I have taken the lyric bird and have examined it.
Said to it,
Go to that woman, blind among roses,
sing to her of their sweetness.
It obeyed me. It sang.
But the woman, something other than flowers obsessed her.
Go through her veins then,
fly up, up into the brain.
Sing to her
to remove her most common problem.
The bird remained silent.

And the lyric bird vomiting into blue air
falls back, its body shivering, wings broken.
Soon the sun will dry it out, insects gather.

DOUBT SHALL NOT MAKE AN END OF YOU

Doubt shall not make an end of you
nor closing eyes lose your shape
when the retina's light fades;
what dawns inside me will light you.

In our public lives we may confine ourselves to darkness,
our nowhere mouths explain away our dreams,
but alone we are incorruptible creatures,
our light sunk too deep to be of any social use
we wander free and perfect without moving

or love on hard carpets
where couples revolving round the room
end found at its centre.

Our love like a whale from its deepest ocean rises—

I offer this and a multitude of images,
from party rooms to oceans,
the single star and all its reflections;
being completed we include all
and nothing wishes to escape us.

Beneath my hand your hardening breast agrees
to sing of its own nature,
then from a place without names our origin comes shivering.

Feel nothing separate then,
we have translated each other into light
and into warmth go streaming.

IN THE DYING OF ANYTHING

Speaking only that our words might bend grasses,
make paths which are both simple and possible,
we talk together and failing with words we touch.
There is nothing simpler nor more human than this.

Once ignorant of any feeling's end
we dreamt in proportion to galaxies,
measuring each other against rainbows love burst,
fell softly soaking us.

But we lie quieter now,
older,
arms pressed out against darkness.
In the dying of anything there walks a creature
        looking for its song:
huge, it bends down planets that it might ask them
the ways back to life again.

No longer one steady and running stream
we are glad to lie here,
catching what life and light we can.
There is nothing simpler, nothing more human than this.

WHERE ALL THE SHIVERING CREATURES

You have become she who walks through places the sun has left
and lights them gently,
whose breasts I trace through loneliness to where
all the shivering creatures of the earth
meet, slow down, touch and soak in the warmth they need
to provide each other with some form of life.

You are she through who I step to touch all mankind,
and the deeper into you I sink the deeper glows elsewhere the
world
and sings of you. It says,
to be touched is the one common miracle.

And our touchings are in no 'dream bower shaded by pines and
silence'
but in streets where the heart pumps out its madness,
where we are not bright solitary creatures
but groups broken ;
at night we wander in each other's shadow.

You are the purpose of my shape,
of this there is no denial,
the most unsociable creature warms his balls against loneliness,
lets his stiff white body remember how once
it sang through tenderness.

Love, unfashionable transitory bird,
It rises above the petrol-tasting sky
The first long held bird note in the babble that follows.

NO MATTER IF YOU REMAIN UNAFFECTED BY

No matter if you remain unaffected by
that animal that makes wars
and sends the smallest child to slaughter
I recognize your shape however sacred burns
and deeper than the lyric bird
lies one dark and gibbering.

And though love sings from a separate source than makes wars
the heart's easily shattered
and pure miracles that once danced through air and frozen time
drain to places where we cannot follow
and love goes limping with its sores.
Our shapes will not stand against the smallest bombs.

As a rabbit stunned by light was I by beauty,
sat glittering inside myself while through the world
deep dwarfs came swarming
and climbed into my dreams—

There are good explosions, but they grow scarce
and deeper than the lyric bird
lies one dark and gibbering.

IN YOUR TURNING AGAINST WALLS

Sitting in a public garden, black coat
around me, the only light that's left
is what lingers in the grass, in lumps of soil,
in fading child voices. Here I wonder
what other lives you are involved in, how
you feel when naked in first visited rooms
you turn, face unfamiliar walls,
cry fake or real as someone enters.
Darling, some lives we pass through we
pass through blindly, echoing
previous attachments; arguing and then silent,
afraid of each other but more afraid
of what the night might not offer us
our boredom contends itself with hurting—
if love is so precious why do we hurt,
twist it to the point of snapping?
Maybe because we grew tired of waking
near bodies so loving we
perverted them with light they could not contain;
crying they gave light back and in receiving found
themselves as small, as incapable of taking.
Once in such gardens I would sit younger,
a private yet open creature,
now it seems any tear's for a larger world
and in your turning against walls I sense
a thousand turnings.
Outside how many windows does the night
harden itself around us? Though our shapes might still
travel through gardens,
though still possible to be gentle,
drowned still in a waterfall of wind and scents,
memory acts as a filter to any new love entering.
Things tighten   skull the dam
the years harden.
That we might burst again—

let oceans flood into us.
Working in earnest against our lives closing down
we write such notes not for one singled out
but for any who on waking find
the landscape grown harder.

WHEN SHE WAKES DRENCHED FROM HER SLEEP

When she wakes drenched from her sleep
She will not ask to be saluted by the light
Nor carolled by morning's squabbling birds,
Nor lying in his arms wish him repeat
the polite conversations already heard;
She'll not be loved by roses but by men,
She will glide free of sweet beauty's net
And all her senses open out
To receive each sensation for herself.
If I could be that real, that open now
And not by half a light half lit
I would not gossip of what is beauty and what is not
Nor reduce love to a freak poem in the dark.

WHEN SNOWMEN KISS OUR BROWS

What shall we be
When snowmen kiss our brows
And the tips of a world have frozen?

What shall we be
Who have no sunlight to melt them,
No
Moon
To guide them?

Something in us is receding.
Not long ago we were more certain,
we were more real.

What can we be
If what we profess to be real
Is a creature still sleeping?

Love come closer to me
Though I will not warm you
I will be real.

What ought we be
When love weakened comes trembling
And touches us
Through vanishing leaves?

Shall we be enemies,
So frightened of each other we jerk alive,
Souls poised upright,
alert in our life's ruins?

or with a common and a human faith
be each other's saviour—
that through walls of flesh we might wander
out into a gleaming world.

THE ICE MAIDEN

Not out of snow or rain frozen,
not out of any of nature's gifts
I made an ice maiden

but it was the lonely freak
walking in my head
that first shaped and loved her.

And now later when cocksure it moves
through pubs through rooms
and stops to glance at her

it sees nothing clear. Only
those who surround her
it sees for what they are.

That she is as ordinary
as all I've touched
will not occur to me;

nor will the fact she needs
only a simple view of me.
I make her huge then, at times

an excuse for the absence
of something larger. Yet this
can hardly matter:

beyond what she is all
is quite similar to her;
falls back into her.

FROM ONE SIDE OF THE MIRROR TO THE OTHER

From one side of the mirror to the other
both afraid of each other's shape
the deep dwarf and lithe boy run
exchanging news about themselves;
And though they both lie and wrestle with their dark
Neither wins and neither's right nor wrong
And their babbling shapes babble on.
From one side of the mirror to the other
squabbling over truth and truth
the deep dwarf and lithe boy run,
and panic if they near themselves.
And though for a while their arguments might warm them
As through the human landscape they limp and trot
Time maps its route to their brains and freezes
helped on by the warmth they've lost;
And caught deep in the chatter they call a mind
The world outside themselves they can't discern
And turning to the mirror grow afraid
When on neither side they find themselves.
From one side of the mirror to the other
both afraid of each other's shape
the deep dwarf and lithe boy run
exchanging views about themselves

SAD ADAM

Sad Adam
Uncurling from a concrete wall
Woken at dawn by rain and sudden ligh
You will move out now
Watching how the trees retreat down avenues of themselves
In your concrete century
Holding some vague idea of the sight you saw
When your eyes first clicked open into paradise

Here it seems
Even the stars are temporary
And the lives that spin beneath them
Rotate without memory.
Of the waiting world.
New Adam
In the markets touching apples
Huge exploding seeds !
Pink mirrors of the barrows !
You come in the brain
when market women offer you warm flowers

Or in rainpark cafés
Your teacup full of leaves
Escaping onto the open lawns
Afraid of the chained pathways
The green notice boards warning against sunset
Sorry for the frightened intruders
The mad dawners escaped from cities
Who pin notes to their bodies then disappear. . . .

Eveless Adam, touching yourself through blue shirts;
Your pale face reflecting in the rain
As the wind blows it passed and shatters it against leaves—
Twenty centuries are nothing here
The sickest headlines disintegrates
The selfish public world is cancelled out.

Yet for all your huge garden
From your own sad body
You cannot escape—
Let it make its own way out then,
Out across parks
And back into cities.
You'll return there coughing up bricks of dust,
Yet from that island you call a soul
Still slow birds will fly out and be evidence
And on the walls of city banks
The memory of a leaf will sing.

ARRIVING AT WINTER

And that one sitting there, talking of trees, of
how damp the autumn forest's grown, even he
is a small wood, and his heart
(sentimental relic though it is)
wanders lost there. Leaves snap; can't even
the trees stand against it?

In the forest we found an angel's body;
its head skinned, the bone opened, thin ice on its brain
preserved tissues, one blade of grass
frozen beneath the whiteness. The night
had been cold. Leaves snap, can't even
the trees stand against it?

In the forest sentimental hunters after light,
butterfly nets at the ready, strut
in marshlands hidden by flower. Leaves snap,
broken by the minds that colour them
according only to their own whims.

My love am I cold that all I say
seems now devoid of you, of how you feel?
Who once sat in sunlight would rather
travel alone. Only in danger does
your life concern me. An inconsistent creature,

between leaves and the shadows they make,
my life moves and in all its space
the world's colours are forming.

ODE ON CELESTIAL MUSIC
(or: *It's The Girl In The Bathroom Singing*)

It's not celestial music it's the girl in the bathroom singing.
You can tell. Although it's winter
the trees outside her window have grown leaves,
all manner of flowers push up through the floorboards.
I think—what a filthy trick that is to play on me,
I snip them with my scissors shouting
'I want only bona fide celestial music!'
Hearing this she stops singing.

Out of her bath now the girl knocks on my door,
'Is my singing disturbing you?' she smiles entering,
'did you say it was licentious or sensual?
And excuse me, my bath towel's slipping.'
A warm and blonde creature
I slam the door on her breasts shouting
'I want only bona fide celestial music!'

Much later on in life I wear my hearing-aid.
What have I done to my body, ignoring it,
splitting things into so many pieces my hands
cannot mend anything. The stars, the buggers, remained silent.
Down in the bathroom now her daughter is singing.
Turning my hearing-aid full volume
I bend close to the floorboards hoping
for at least one flower to appear.

THE NECESSARY SLAUGHTER

There was a bird come recently. When I went into my room
I saw it balanced on the open window.
It was a thin bird, I dreamt worms for it
And in the morning it was fatter.
And the next night for the worms
I dreamt rich soil, and then other creatures,
those that could not fly but now had ground on which to walk
all came and waited round my bed.
I dreamt for them what they needed,
The bird the worm, the fox the hen, etc., etc.
right up to the two-legged creature.
Sadly the more they came the more
I had to dream for them each other's murder
Till my dreams became a planet and that planet called
The necessary slaughter.

A SMALL DRAGON

I've found a small dragon in the woodshed.
Think it must have come from deep inside a forest
because it's damp and green and leaves
are still reflecting in its eyes.

I fed it on many things, tried grass,
the roots of stars, hazel-nut and dandelion,
but it stared up at me as if to say, I need
foods you can't provide.

It made a nest among the coal,
not unlike a bird's but larger,
it is out of place here
and is quite silent.

If you believed in it I would come
hurrying to your house to let you share my wonder,
but I want instead to see
if you yourself will pass this way.

BOMBSCARE

Without much effort the piece of earth I was sitting on
broke off like fruit-cake from the ground
and drifted out of what we call the world.
Fortunately I had my winter clothes on,
for with every star I pass I'm growing colder,
it's a wonderous and amazing sight to see them pass
like bubbles in clear water.

I did not set out on this journey alone;
there were some picnickers here but they seemed
to shrink and disappear. Funny, they seemed
quite like myself at first.

Still there are some creatures here,
rabbits, squirrels, a few gibbering hares,
we join in a circle to keep warm
and as each fails and dies I take their fur
and bury myself beneath it.

If you see my shadow drift across your lawn,
the shadow of a man in winter clothes
sitting on a lump of soil,
you're bound to be amazed, but do not phone
an ambulance or a fire-brigade;
even helicopters could not reach me,
and spaceships I fear are too expensive.

Now I've grown used to it and as I said
with every star I pass I'm growing colder;
it's funny how the worlds are made
and how some pass through bombscare to laughter.

THE FAWN DREAMS OF BLOND CREATURES

Once it slept there quiet; sunlight
drunk in the forest, in no hurry to fade
played with its sleep, fell around it,
that fawn, tired, in whose belly
the sun was setting.
And during the night while it and we
were sleeping something came here,
hunters whose feet left boils on the grass, came
here. From pools in some clearings
night mares lifted their heads, sniffed
our sleep. It was heavy, deep. Forests
faded from the fawn's brain.

It woke in a bus terminus. One leaf
squashed against wheels. Out into
the city, yawning and puzzled perhaps
in its eyes some kind of fright; moving
among thin blond creatures, moving
simply that. How the gardens
seem charred, burnt by the lack of sun
in the blond creatures' bellies.
And how the huge posts are branchless;
the soil itself buried.
Sad to have woken from forests into this.
Then move out to the suburbs where

now some trace of green shows, now
the thinning of sounds, now at least
some trees; fields. Yet here still
into the wet distance the silver
branchless posts wandering, void of birds.

Evening and the night mares trotting
back to silence; not one sunbeam
left uncut by stone. Into the parks then,
then across the iced lakes
late children have hurried from.

To stop; shivering by rain shelters,
near the young virgins untangled now
from sadness—of all blond creatures only
these do not frighten, only these
breath warm in the fawn's brain.
And how easily the park paths split, snap
into sections of colour, how
easily in oceans of greyness these
blond creatures roam, move back
towards gates; and how easily
above treescapes the fawn smells black
smoke drifting. In the wind rubbing
against it, in the wind caught
on its eyelids, in the wind in its mouth
it tastes worlds mixing. Already
on its waking dark ice has settled.

A WESTERN TALE

I have reached the end of the first or last prairie
(depending on how you look at things) and
stand watching the rain
teem on the river. My horse has wandered away,
I'm too tired to go find it; been riding all night
watching the boat through the trees.
It's much closer now. The dawn
smells of gunsmoke and timber.
I've an old bullet in me, how long
it has been there
I cannot remember. Here comes the boat
on the teeming river. How long
it has teemed here I cannot remember.

YOU'D BETTER BELIEVE HIM
A Fable

Discovered an old rocking-horse in Woolworth's,
He tried to feed it but without much luck
So he stroked it, had a long conversation about
The trees it came from, the attics it had visited.
Tried to take it out then
But the store detective he
Called the store manager who
Called the police who in court next morning said
'He acted strangely when arrested,
His statement read simply "I believe in rocking-horses".
We have reason to believe him mad.'
'Quite so,' said the prosecution,
'Bring in the rocking horse as evidence.'
'I'm afraid it's escaped sir,' said the store manager,
'Left a hoof-print as evidence
On the skull of the store detective.'
'Quite so,' said the prosecution, fearful
of the neighing
Out in the corridor.

AND THE KEEPER OF THE IRON GARDEN

And the keeper of the iron garden has grown too dull to bother
moving from his bed among the rusting flowers
and the rain teeming onto him is another planet's sorrow
and his heart growing cold among the overgrown bushes
and his eyes locked in the tool-shed are decaying
and there is only the feel of the wind
and what scent it brings to remind him
of less terrible worlds.

And the dwarfs in the iron garden have grown flesh and moved
away
and the statues have found less naked positions
and the children coming giggling
and the old photographers hiding in the ruins
arrange them in pornographic positions to suit
the shape of the world.